D1597838

Wolfgang Amadeus Mozart

Complete Sonatas and Variations for Violin and Piano

From the Breitkopf & Härtel Complete Works Edition

SERIES I

DOVER PUBLICATIONS, INC., *New York*

Published in Canada by General Publishing Company, Ltd., 30 Lesmill Road, Don Mills, Toronto, Ontario.

Published in the United Kingdom by Constable and Company, Ltd., 3 The Lanchesters, 162–164 Fulham Palace Road, London W6 9ER.

This Dover edition, first published in 1992, is a republication of portions of Vols. I and II of Series 18: *Sonaten und Variationen für Pianoforte und Violine* from *Wolfgang Amadeus Mozart's Werke. Kritisch durchgesehene Gesammt-ausgabe*, originally published by Breitkopf & Härtel, Leipzig, in 1879.

Manufactured in the United States of America
Dover Publications, Inc., 31 East 2nd Street, Mineola, N.Y. 11501

Library of Congress Cataloging-in-Publication Data

Mozart, Wolfgang Amadeus, 1756–1791.
   [Violin, piano music]
   Complete sonatas and variations for violin and piano : from the Breitkopf & Härtel complete works edition / Wolfgang Amadeus Mozart.
   1 score (2 v.)
   Reprint. Originally published: Leipzig : Breitkopf & Härtel, 1879 (from Wolfgang Amadeus Mozart's Werke. Kritisch durchgesehene Gesammtaus-gabe. Series 18, v. 1–2: Sonaten und Variationen für Pianoforte und Violine).
   Series 1 contains sonatas K. 6–15, 26–31, 296, 301–306, 372; Series 2 contains sonatas K. 376–380, 402–404, 454, 481, 526, 547, Variations on La bergère Célimène, K. 359, and Variations on Hélas, j'ai perdu mon amant, K. 360.
   ISBN 0-486-27299-0 (Series 1). — ISBN 0-486-27406-3 (Series 2)
   1. Sonatas (Violin and piano) 2. Variations (Violin and piano) I. Mozart, Wolfgang Amadeus, 1756–1791. Sonatas, violin, piano. 1992. II. Mozart, Wolfgang Amadeus, 1756–1791. Variationen über La bergère Célimène. 1992. III. Mozart, Wolfgang Amadeus, 1756–1791. Variationen über Hélas, j'ai perdu mon amant. 1992.
M218.M75C6 1992   92-757257
                                                       CIP

                                                       M

Contents

V = not in Sch

disc
K 57
58
60

Complete Sonatas and Variations for Violin and Piano

SERIES I

Violin Sonata in C Major, K.6

Andante.

Menuetto primo.

Menuetto secondo.

Menuetto primo da Capo.

Allegro molto.

10   *Sonata in C Major, K.6*

Violin Sonata in D Major, K.7

Adagio.

Menuetto primo.

Menuetto secondo.

Violin Sonata in B-flat Major, K.8

Menuetto primo.

Menuetto secondo.

Menuetto primo da Capo.

Violin Sonata in G Major, K.9

Menuetto primo..

Menuetto secondo.

Menuetto primo da Capo al Fine

Violin Sonata in B-flat Major, K.10

MENUETTO PRIMO.

MENUETTO SECONDO.

Menuetto primo da Capo.

Violin Sonata in G Major, K.11

MENUETTO.

Da capo Alleg:

Violin Sonata in A Major, K.12

Violin Sonata in F Major, K.13

Sonata in F Major, K.13   59

MENUETTO PRIMO.

MENUETTO SECONDO.

Menuetto primo da Capo

Violin Sonata in C Major, K.14

Sonata in C Major, K.14

Menuetto primo.

legato

Menuetto secondo en Carillon.

Menuetto primo da capo.

Violin Sonata in B-flat Major, K.15

Allegro grazioso.

Violin Sonata in E-flat Major, K.26

Adagio poco Andante.

Violin Sonata in G Major, K.27

Allegro.

88   *Sonata in G Major, K.27*

Violin Sonata in C Major, K.28

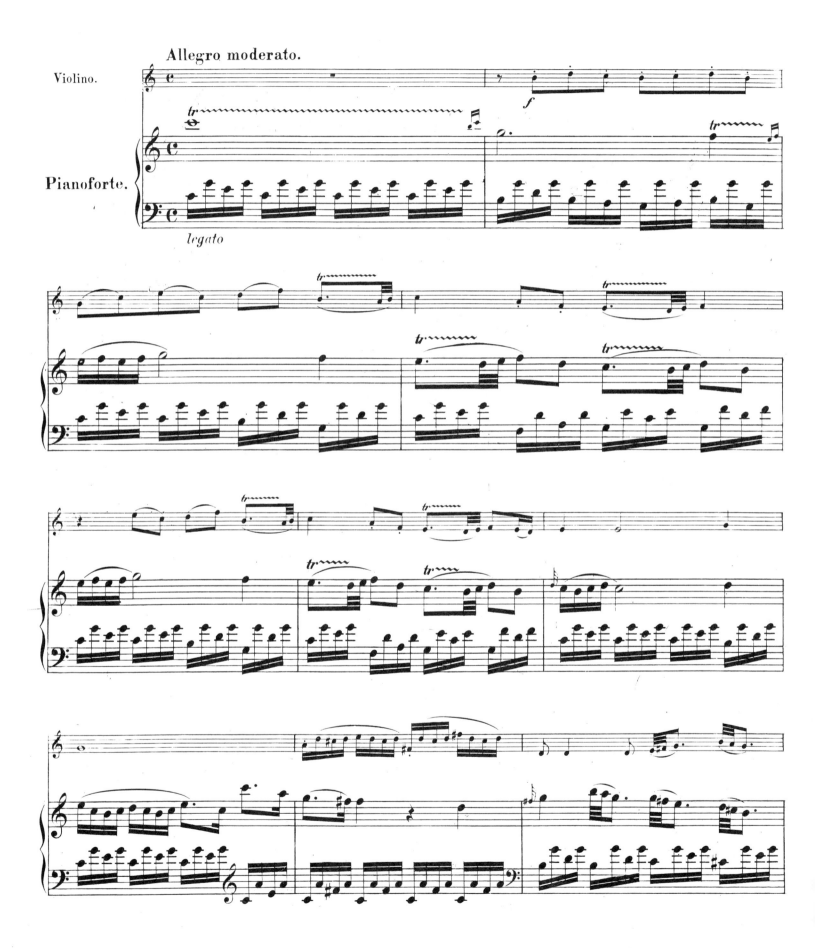

Violin Sonata in D Major, K.29

Trio.

Violin Sonata in F Major, K.30

Rondo.
Tempo di Menuetto.

Violin Sonata in B-flat Major, K.31

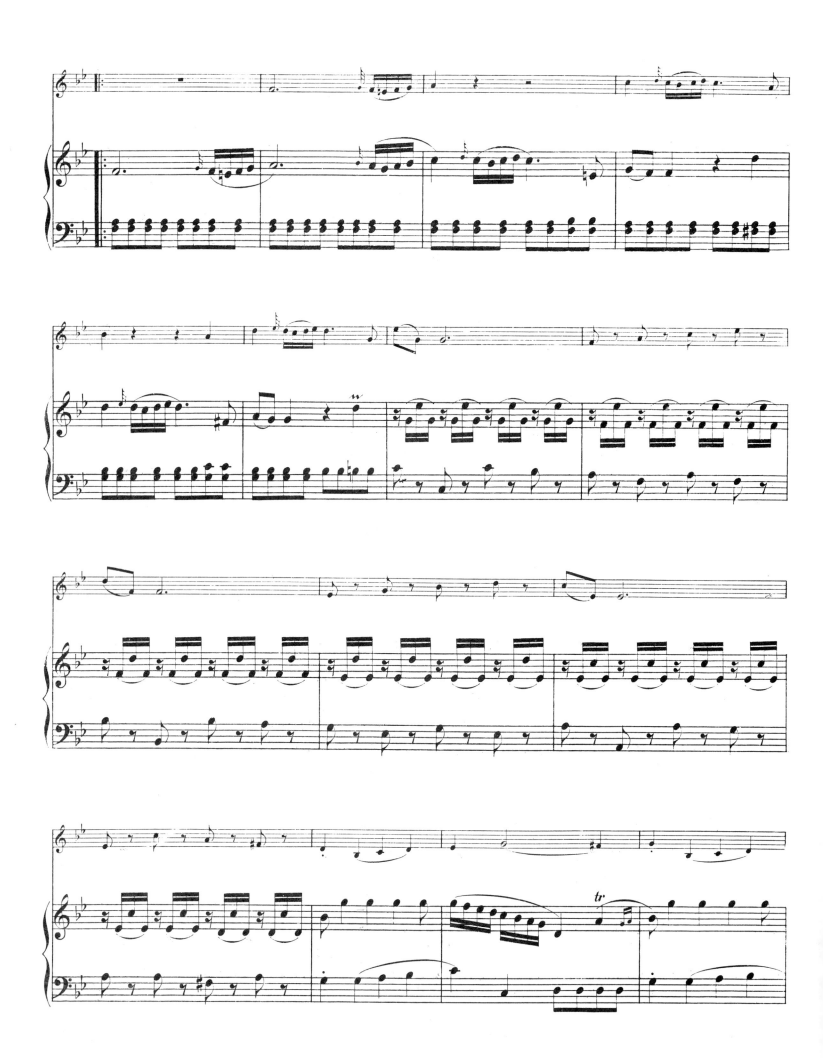

Violin Sonata in C Major, K.296

RONDO.
Allegro.

Sonata in C Major, K.296

Violin Sonata in G Major, K.301/293a

Allegro.

Violin Sonata in E-flat Major, K.302/293b

Rondo.
Andante grazioso.

Violin Sonata in C Major, K.303/293c

Violin Sonata in E Minor, K.304/300c

Violin Sonata in A Major, K.305/293d

VAR.III.

Violin Sonata in D Major, K.306/300 l

Allegretto.

Allegretto.

Allegro.

Allegro assai.

Sonata in D Major, K.306/300l 207

Violin Sonata in B-flat Major, K.372

From here on, completed
by Abbé Stadler.

Mozart
Sonata in E Minor, K. 60
Violin

CD Sheet Music™

1

Rondo
Tempo di Menuetto

CD Sheet Music

CD Sheet Music

CD Sheet Music™

Mozart
Sonata in Eb Major, K. 58
Violin

1

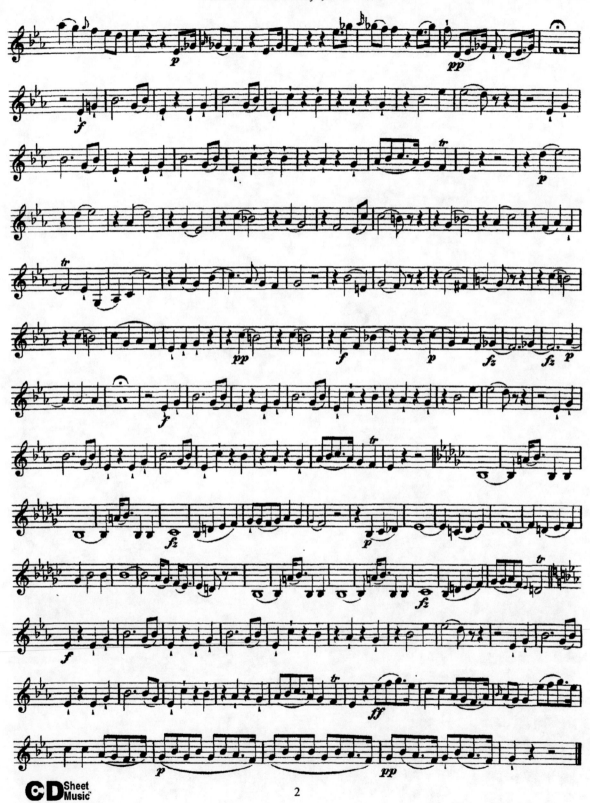

CD Sheet Music

CD Sheet Music™

Mozart
Sonata in F Major, K. 57
Violin

Menuetto da capo

1

CD Sheet Music

CD Sheet Music

CD Sheet Music™

Mozart
Sonata in F Major, K. 57

1

Menuetto

Mozart—Sonata in F Major, K. 57

Menuetto da capo

CD Sheet Music

CD Sheet Music

CD Sheet Music™

CD Sheet Music™

Mozart—Sonata in F Major, K. 57

CD Sheet Music

CD Sheet Music

CD Sheet Music™

CD Sheet Music